Secrets Of Managing Budgets

What IT Managers Need To Know In Order To Understand How Their Company Uses Money

"Practical, proven techniques that will help you to manage your IT Manager budget successful"

Dr. Jim Anderson

Published by
Blue Elephant Consulting
Tampa, Florida

Printed in the United States of America

Library of Congress Control Number: 2015916950

ISBN-13: 978-1517782313

ISBN-10: 1517782317

Warning – Disclaimer

The purpose of this book is to educate and entertain. This book does not promise or guarantee that anyone following the ideas, tips, suggestions, techniques or strategies will be successful. The author, publisher and distributor(s) shall have neither liability nor responsibility to anyone with respect to any loss or damage caused, or alleged to be caused, directly or indirectly by the information contained in this book.

Recent Books By The Author

Product Management

- Product Management Secrets: Techniques For Product Managers To Boost Product Sales And Increase Customer Satisfaction

- Customer Lessons For Product Managers: Techniques For Product Managers To Better Understand What Their Customers Really Want

Public Speaking

- Secrets To Organizing A Speech For Maximum Impact: How to put together a speech that will capture and hold your audience's attention

- How To Become A Better Speaker By Changing How You Speak: Change techniques that will transform a speech into a memorable event

CIO Skills

- What CIOs Need To Know About Working With Partners: Techniques For CIOs To Use In Order To Be Able To Successfully Work With Partners

- How CIOs Can Make Innovation Happen: Tips And Techniques For CIOs To Use In Order To Make Innovation Happen In Their IT Department

IT Manager Skills

- Growing Your CIO Career: How CIOs Can Work With The Entire Company In Order To Be Successful

- How IT Managers Can Make Innovation Happen: Tips And Techniques For IT Managers To Use In Order To Make Innovation Happen In Their Teams

Negotiating

- Learn How To Package Trades In Your Next Negotiation

- Learn How To Signal In Your Next Negotiation: How To Develop The Skill Of Effective Signaling In A Negotiation In Order To Get The Best Possible Outcome

Miscellaneous

- The Internet-Enabled Successful School District Superintendent: How To Use The Internet To Boost Parental Involvement In Your Schools

- Power Distribution Unit (PDU) Secrets: What Everyone Who Works In A Data Center Needs To Know!

Note: See a complete list of books by Dr. Jim Anderson at the back of this book.

<u>Acknowledgements</u>

Any book like this one is the result of years of real-world work experience. In my over 25 years of working for 7 different firms, I have met countless fantastic people and I've been mentored by some truly exceptional ones. Although I've probably forgotten some of the people who made me the person that I am today, here is my attempt to finally give them the recognition that they so truly deserve:

- Thomas P. Anderson
- Art Puett
- Bobbi Marshall
- Bob Boggs

Dr. Jim Anderson

5

This book is dedicated to my wife Lori. None of this would have been possible without her love and support.

Thanks for the best 24 years of my life (so far)...!

Speaking.   Negotiating.   Managing.   Marketing.

Table Of Contents

Why Do CIOs Need Business Skills?

An IT manager's budget controls what he or she and their team are going to be able to accomplish this year. No, creating a budget may not be the most enjoyable thing that you'll be called on to do, but it just might be the most important. The challenge that a lot of IT managers have when it comes to creating a good budget is that it requires them to master a number of terms and concepts that they may have never encountered in school.

The good news is that you are not the first IT manager to create a budget. There is a great deal to learn from the tips that other managers can provide you with. A good guide for how you should create your budget may be provided by your company's financial statements.

In order to understand the company's financial situation you'll need to master the company's balance sheet. Additionally you'll have to understand the company's assets and its liabilities. How the company runs its day-to-day operations are closely tied to its use of working capital and so you'll need to have an understanding of this also.

The company will be funding new IT projects using financial leverage and so you need to understand how this financial tool works. The status of the company is closely watched by outsiders and in order to keep your team informed you are going to have to learn how to read an income statement and a cash flow statement.

Your company will be making an investment in your IT team and they expect it to return a profit. This means that you need to understand terms like ROI, net present value, and internal rate of return in order to understand how your performance is going to be measured. Master these financial terms and you'll be ready to create a complete budget for you and your team.

One way to think about your IT budget is as fuel in the tank of your IT team. The more that you have, the farther you can go. Read on and find out how to fill your tank up…!

For more information on what it takes to be a great IT Manager, check out my blog, **The Accidental IT Leader**, at:

www.TheAccidentalITLeader.com

Good luck!

-   Dr. Jim Anderson

About The Author

I must confess that I never set out to be a CIO. When I went to school, I studied Computer Science and thought that I'd get a nice job programming and that would be that. Well, at least part of that plan worked out!

My first job was working for Boeing on their F/A-18 fighter jet program. I spent my days programming fighter jet software in assembly language and I loved it. The U.S. government decided to save some money and went looking for other countries to sell this plane to. This put me into an unfamiliar role: I started to meet with foreign military officials and I ended up having to manage groups of engineers who were working on international projects.

Time moved on and so did I. I found myself working for Siemens, the big German telecommunications company. They were making phone switches and selling them to the seven U.S. phone companies. The problem was that the switches were too complicated. Customers couldn't tell the difference between one complicated phone switch from another complicated phone switch. Once again I found myself working with the sales and marketing teams to find ways to make the great technology that the engineers had developed understandable to both internal and external customers.

I've spent over 25 years working as an senior IT professional for both big companies and startups. This has given me an opportunity to learn what it takes to manage and IT department in ways that allow it to maximize its output while becoming a valuable part of the overall company.

I now live in Tampa Florida where I spend my time managing my consulting business, Blue Elephant Consulting, teaching college courses at the University of South Florida, and traveling to work with companies like yours to share the knowledge that I have about how to create and manage successful IT departments.

I'm always available to answer questions and I can be reached at:

Dr. Jim Anderson
Blue Elephant Consulting
Email: jim@BlueElephantConsulting.com
Facebook: http://goo.gl/1TVoK
Web: http://www.BlueElephantConsulting.com/

"Unforgettable communication skills that will set your ideas free..."

Create IT Departments That Are Productive And A Valuable Asset To The Rest Of The Company !

Dr. Jim Anderson is available to provide training and coaching on the topics that are the most important to people who have to manage IT departments: how can I build a productive IT department (and keep it together) while at the same time providing the rest of the company with the IT services that they need?

Dr. Anderson believes that in order to both learn and remember what he says, speakers need to laugh. Each one of his speeches is full of fun and humor so that what he says "sticks" with everyone.

Dr. Anderson's CIO SkillsTraining Includes:

1. How to identify and attract the right type of IT workers to your IT department.
2. How to build relationships with the company's senior management in order to get the support that you need?
3. How to stay on top of changing technology and security issues so that you never get surprised?

Dr. Jim Anderson works with over 100 customers per year. To invite Dr. Anderson to work with you, contact him at:

Phone: 813-418-6970 or
Email: jim@BlueElephantConsulting.com

Blue
Elephant
Consulting

Speaking. Negotiating. Managing. Marketing.

10

12

Chapter 1

IT Manager Tips For Creating An Effective Budget

Chapter1: IT Manager Tips For Creating An Effective Budget

Look, as an IT manager you have to create an annual budget for your IT team so just get over it. Since you have to do it, it sure seems like you'd want to find ways to turn this chore into **a team building and planning tool**. If this sounds like a good idea to you, then we're going to have to have a talk about just exactly how you can show some leadership and go about making this happen.

Don't Try To Do It All Yourself

Creating a budget is a big job for any IT manager to take on. If you try to do it all yourself, you may be able to pull it off, but it's going to crush you. **You won't be able to get anything else done** during the time that you're working on creating the budget.

A better approach it to reach out to your IT team and **ask for volunteers**. Point out to everyone that by helping you complete tasks such as doing research for various budgetary line items, they can gain valuable insights into how the company's budgeting process works.

Be Smart About Reducing Costs

It is entirely possible that after you've put your budget together, you'll sit back and realize that **the costs that are associated with your budget are too high**. When you have this realization, it's going to be time to do some cost cutting.

How you actually go about doing the cost cutting is where the magic happens. It can be all too easy to just start lopping a percentage off of each area of your budget. Instead, take a look at what your budget is being spent on. Identify the activities that your team will be engaging in that **add value for the customer** (and which ones don't). Cut the non-value activities first.

Show How Your Budget Generates Income

At the end of the day, the reason that your management is willing to give your IT team money in the first place is **so that the company can make more money**. It is going to be your responsibility to use your budget to show them how this is going to happen.

In order to accomplish this, you are going to have to understand just exactly **how the company views your budget**. It's not so much a request on your part for funding, but rather a request for the company to invest in your team in order to generate a specific return.

What All Of This Means For You

Your IT dream team's annual budget is a very powerful tool that you can use to **control what the team works on** and what they are able to accomplish this year. In order to do it effectively, you are going to have to keep a few things in mind as you create the budget.

Creating a budget can be a big task – it will eat up all of your time if you aren't careful. Ask for volunteers to help get work done. If you have to cut costs, take the time to make sure you know what activities will add value for the end user and don't cut those ones. Finally, make sure that you'll be able to show how your budget generates income for the company.

Nobody ever said that this budget creation thing was going to be easy to do! However, if you take the time to do it correctly and you make sure that it is in alignment with its environment, then **you'll have a powerful tool** with which to become a successful IT manager.

Chapter 2

Why IT Managers Need To Care About Financial Statements

Chapter 2: Why IT Managers Need To Care About Financial Statements

We've probably all heard about **financial statements**, but have you ever really sat down and taken a close look at one? If you haven't, then you should! The reason is that financial statements are how the leadership that runs your company talks about how the company is doing. If you want to speak their language, then we'd better take a look at what you're going to have to learn...

Why Do Financial Statements Matter?

I can almost see you saying to yourself, **why should I care** about my company's financial statements. I mean, you've seen those statements before and they pretty much look like they are written in Greek. Why bother?

The answer is that your career depends on it. The ability to both read a financial statement and to understand what it is saying to you **has become a critical IT manager skill** ever since decision making authority started getting pushed down the line a few years ago. Your management wants you to know about this stuff and your IT team needs you to know about this stuff.

By reading your company's financial statements you'll be able to determine what the company owns, what it owes to other firms, where its money comes from and where it spends it, how much profit the firm is making, and what kind of financial health the company is in. Ultimately, financial statements **form the vocabulary** that the people running the company use to talk about the company – sounds like that is a good language for you to know.

The 3 Types Of Financial Statements

In the U.S., the Securities and Exchange Commission requires publically traded companies to create and file 3 different financial documents on a regular basis. Privately traded firms don't have to file these same documents, but more often than not **their investors require that the documents be created** so that they can determine the health of the company.

The three types of financial statements that firms use to report on the state of their business are: **the balance sheet, the income statement, and the cash flow statement**. These three documents are used by multiple parties (managers, shareholders, and outside investors) to determine the state of the business.

No matter what type of company you work for, the firm's 3 types of financial statements **are always going to follow the same general format**. There will be differences in the specific line items that your firm reports, but overall the 3 statements will be similar enough to the ones produced by other firms so that you can compare companies.

What Does All Of This Mean For You?

As an IT manager, you've probably gotten this far in your career based on your technical knowledge. Congratulations. Now it's time to move on. Financial statements **hold the key to understanding** where the company has been and where it is going. This is information that you're going to have to be able to understand in order to properly manage your IT dream team.

The reason that financial statements are so important is because the need to be able to read and understand a financial statement **has become very important** as organizations have pushed decision making authority farther down. You'll need to be able to understand the three types of financial statements: the balance sheet, the income sheet, and the cash-flow sheet.

An IT manager who is comfortable reading financial statements **is an asset to the company**. Get good at doing this and you'll be ready for the next step in your career.

Chapter 3

An IT Manager's New Best Friend: The Company Balance Sheet

Chapter 3: An IT Manager's New Best Friend: The Company Balance Sheet

Hey IT manager, **how is that company that you are working for currently doing?** Yeah, yeah – I know that all of the press releases that your management keeps putting out say that things have never been better and the internal emails that you get from the big guy say the same thing. However, how are things really going? It turns out that you can answer this question if you know how to read your company's balance sheet...

What Is A Balance Sheet?

One of the biggest questions that both investors and IT managers always ask about a company is **"how is it doing?"** Answering this question can be complicated, but one way to start to get a handle on it is to take a look at the company's numbers: what is their current financial position?

The balance sheet is designed to an answer to this question. It **summarizes the company's financial position** at the end of a time period: month, quarter, or year. The balance sheet describes the assets that the company controls and documents how those assets are financed.

The 3 Parts To A Balance Sheet

Every balance sheet is designed to document how a company is providing a solution to **the classic accounting equation:**

Assets = Liabilities + Owner's Equity

Perhaps we should spend just a moment talking about what each of these **three components** actually are.

The easiest one is **Assets**. An asset is something that the company has decided to invest in so that they can conduct business. If the company was a newspaper publisher, then a printing press would be one of their assets. Assets can also consist of cash and financial instruments along with inventories of raw materials and even finished goods. The list can be rounded out by including land, buildings, and equipment.

Next comes **Liabilities**. The money that was used to obtain the assets that the company uses had to come from somewhere. If the company borrowed money or made arrangements to pay suppliers for goods and services, then this money that they owe is called a liability.

Finally, **Owner's Equity** is what would be left over after the company's total liabilities were deducted from the company's assets. One way of thinking about the owner's equity is if the company was sold off today, how much would the owners walk away with?

The balance sheet **"balances" a company's assets and its liabilities**. It shows you how much it has invested in assets and just exactly where the money has been invested. A balance sheet will show you how the company has paid for its assets: did it borrow money or did it spend the owner's investment?

By itself, a single balance sheet is only so useful. However, when **compared to a balance sheet for a period in the past**, a balance sheet can reveal a great deal about how well a company is managing its assets.

What All Of This Means For You

As an IT manager, you have an obligation to know **how the firm that you are working for is currently doing**. This obligation comes about because you need to be able to manage your career as well as to show some leadership and be able to answer company related questions for your team.

The company's balance sheet is a key part of **how you'll understand how the company is doing at any point in time**. The balance sheet will show you the company's assets, liabilities, and owner's equity.

Using the current balance sheet, you'll be able to compare the company's performance to previous years. Ultimately this will tell you and your IT dream team **how you can expect your IT manager career to proceed** where you are currently working.

Chapter 4

Assets & Liabilities: What Does An IT Manager Need To Know?

Table 24.3 : SUMMARY BALANCE SHEET

Aim	Item	A Annual Costs in £m	B Annual Costs in £m	C Annual Costs in £m	D Annual Costs in £m
	Selected Real Costs Incurred in 2001				
ECONOMY	Road Provision	24.73	23.14	24.45	23.95
	Parking Provision	0.26	0.70	0.75	0.76
	Public Transport Provision	4.74	4.76	5.09	4.92
	New Drainage Provision	1.49	1.81	1.86	1.64
	Gas, Water and Electricity Provision	13.42	13.04	13.42	13.43
	Total Selected Real Costs Incurred in 2001	44.64	43.45	45.57	44.70
	Imputed Costs Incurred in 2001				
	User Costs of Public and Private Travel	166.76	164.97	166.47	166.68
	Economy Sub-total	211.40	208.42	212.04	211.38
CONSERVATION (Part)	Effects of Road Traffic Noise	0.61	0.55	0.63	0.54
	Loss of Benefit from Rural and Urban land	4.30	4.37	4.44	4.22
	Loss of Agricultural Viability	0.20	0.13	0.10	0.22
	Residential and Agricultural Disturbance Loss	1.26	1.20	1.24	1.12
	Conservation Cost Sub-total	6.37	6.25	6.41	6.10
	Total Imputed Costs Incurred in 2001	173.13	171.22	172.88	172.78

Chapter 4: Assets & Liabilities: What Does An IT Manager Need To Know?

As an IT manager, you have a responsibility to your team to be able to keep them informed on the economic health of the company. Every company goes through periods of ups and downs, boom and bust, economic results. Your responsibility is to be able to **understand what the company's current financial situation is** no matter what the current management is or is not saying and to be able to show some leadership and be able to clearly explain it to your IT team. This means that you're going to have to have a good understanding of just exactly what assets and liabilities are.

What Are Assets?

Your company's financial statement **starts with a listing of its assets**. Remember that assets are things that the company invests in so that it can make money. On the financial statement, the assets that can be most easily converted into cash will be listed first. This will include such things as cash on hand, marketable securities, receivables, and inventory. Grouped together, these are called "current assets".

A good way to think about **current assets** is to view them as being assets that can be converted into cash within one year.

The next items listed under assets on the company's financial statement are what are called the **"fixed assets"**. These are assets that would be tougher to convert into cash. This can include such things as buildings and equipment.

One final note on fixed assets. As a general rule, these types of assets **depreciate over time** (become less valuable because of wear and tear) and so the company will keep track of how much their value has been decreased by a term called "accumulated depreciation".

What Are Liabilities?

The other side of the coin when you are talking about assets are liabilities. Liabilities are money that is owed to creditors. The claims of creditors that typically must be repaid within a year are called **"current liabilities"**.

If you subtract the company's current liabilities from its current assets you end up with what is called the company's **"net working capital"**. This is how much money the company has tied up in its short-term operating activities.

Every company also has what are called **"long-term liabilities"**. These include such things as bonds and mortgages. If you subtract the company's total liabilities from the company's total assets you end up with the owner's equity. This is also referred to as being the "retained earnings".

What Does All Of This Mean To You?

IT managers have a responsibility to be able to explain the current state of the company to their IT teams. This means that IT managers who want to be able to understand their company's financial statements need to **start with an understanding of what assets and liabilities are**.

Assets are things that the company **invests in so that it can make money**. On a financial statement assets are listed in the order in which they can be converted into money. Liabilities are money that is owed to creditors. On a financial statement liabilities are listed in terms of both short term current liabilities and long term liabilities.

No, an IT manager does not have to become an accountant in order to understand the company's financial statements. However, a knowledge of some of **the basic terms** is required so that you'll be able to ensure that your IT dream team knows what's going on with the company.

Chapter 5

What IT Managers Need To Know About Working Capital

Chapter 5: What IT Managers Need To Know About Working Capital

Have you ever wondered how your company pays its bills? I mean, every day when you come to work, the lights are on, the security guard is working, and food is served in the cafeteria. Somehow, thanks to the efforts of your company's leadership, **that is all getting paid for**, but how? The secret my dear IT manager lies in the world of working capital...

What Is Working Capital?

We've all probably heard of "capital" and "working capital" before, but what is it? In short, working capital is the amount of money that a company **has available to spend today**. A fancy way of saying this is that working capital is a company's liquid finances – it can get its hands on it right now.

You would think that **having more working capital** than less would always be a good thing, right? Well, yes and no. Clearly having access to too little working capital can put a company in a bad position – management may not be able to pay their bills. However, at the same time having too much working capital may result in the company having to pay financing costs (that working capital had to come from somewhere).

The Impact Of Inventory?

All too often working capital is not just laying around at a firm in the form of piles of cash. Although that sure would be nice. Instead, it's often **tied up in the company's inventory**. This may go a long way to explain why so many of the projects that your IT dream team works on have to do with inventories. Just like working capital, a company doesn't want to have either too much or too little inventory.

The balance here is that if a company carries a lot of inventory **they can quickly fill customer orders**. That is a good thing. However, having a lot of inventory also means that any unsold goods are getting older every day that they sit on the company's warehouse shelves. Depending on how fast things change in the industry that your company competes in, the value of the items in your company's inventory may be decreasing by as much as 2% per day!

What All Of This Means For You

Just like a car that needs to have gas in its tank in order to be able to go anywhere, a company needs to have working capital **in order to pay its bills**. Careful management of this valuable resource is required in order to ensure that the company does not have either too much or too little of it.

One of the key areas where working capital will show up in any company is **in its inventory**. Much of what an IT team is called on to do will probably have something to do with managing or tracking the company's inventory.

Realizing **the importance of working capital** is something that every IT manager needs to do. This understanding can go a long way in making sure that you are able to grasp the motivation behind decisions that your upper management makes.

Chapter 6

IT Managers Need To Know About Financial Leverage

Chapter 6: IT Managers Need To Know About Financial Leverage

As an IT manager you are going to want to be able to show some leadership and be able to have intelligent conversations with the people who are running your company. More often than not, those people are either going to be working in the company's finance department or they are going to have a finance background. This all means that your management is going to be using big words like **"leverage"** that you're going to have to understand. Let's do something about that right now.

What Is "Leverage"?

If you've watched any movie in the past few years that dealt with a business or money, then undoubtedly you've heard the actors use the phrase "...he's highly leveraged..." This leads to the question: what are they talking about? In the world of business, financial leverage refers to the act of **borrowing money so that you can acquire an asset**. When somebody (or some company) is highly leveraged, then they've acquired an asset using more of someone else's money than their own.

You don't want to get this kind of leverage confused with another type: operating leverage. **Operating leverage** is talking about the extent to which a company's operating costs are fixed versus variable.

How Do Companies Use Leverage?

Borrowing money is a bad idea, right? Isn't this what all of our parents told us as we were growing up? Well, it turns out that when used correctly, leverage is **a very powerful business tool** that can help your IT dream team do more projects.

Let's say that your company wanted to implement an IT program that was going to cost $1,000,000. Your company contributes $200,000 and borrows $800,000 to fund the project. A year goes by after the project has been implemented and your company has generated an extra $2,000,000 in profits because of the project. Ignore the cost of borrowing the money and assume that the company repays the borrowed $800,000. This leaves the company with **$1,800,000 in profits** after they repay themselves for funding the project. Clearly using leverage really paid off in this situation.

What Does All Of This Mean For You?

Financial leverage is a technique that companies use in order to implement projects that they don't currently have enough funding to do by themselves. This is **a powerful technique** that comes with some risks.

Firms borrow money, leverage, and combine it with their own money to fund activities that they want to perform. Assuming that the value of the activity increases, then the firm can repay the borrowed funds and will emerge with **more funds than they had when they began**. If the activity decreases in value, then the firm will end up losing money.

Using leverage can allow a firm to perform more IT projects and to start them sooner than if they didn't. However, the use of leverage puts the entire firm at risk of not being able to repay its loans. IT managers need to understand how this **powerful financing technique** works and what they need to keep an eye on when it's being used.

Chapter 7

IT Managers Need To Make Friends With The Company's Income Statement

Chapter 7: IT Managers Need To Make Friends With The Company's Income Statement

So IT manager, how is your company doing? Are they going to be able to fund your IT dream team's projects this year? Will there be any money left over for your management to hand out as bonuses to your IT team in order to make sure that they stay on board and don't bail? The best way to find out **how your company is doing** is to show some leadership and take a look at its income statement. Let's make sure that you know how to read it.

The Income Statement

Say hello to an IT manager's new best friend: **the Income Statement**. An income statement shows the results of your company's operations over a specified period of time. This is an important point: the balance sheet provides a snapshot of the company's status at a given point in time. However, the income statement shows the company's results within a defined period of time. This period is generally at the end of a month, a quarter, or at the end of the year.

So what does an income statement show? It shows you **if your company is making a profit** – if the revenue that it is taking in is greater than its costs and expenses. This is why the income statement is sometimes referred to as the "Profit and Loss Statement" or more simply the "P&L ".

Since the income statement tells you if your company was profitable at the end of a period, this allows you to answer other questions also. From the information contained in a balance sheet you'll be able to determine how much money

your company had to spend in order to make the profit that it made. This means that you'll be able to calculate the company's profit margin.

How To Make Sense Of The Income Statement

The income statement's contents can be represented by **a simple equation**:

$$\text{Revenues} - \text{Expenses} = \text{Net Income (or Net Loss)}$$

The company's revenues represent the money that the company has made from **selling products or services to customers**. The various costs and expenses that the company incurred in generating these revenues are then deducted from its revenues. What is left over is called the net income.

When taking a look at a company's income statement, it is most helpful if you do it in **a multiperiod format**. Only by doing it this way will you be able to spot trends and turnarounds.

What All Of This Means For You

Every publically traded company (and a number of private firms) creates an **income statement**. This statement shows the results of the company's operations over some period of time.

IT managers need to know how to read an income statement in order to be able to **understand how their company is doing**. The income statement shows the company's revenues as well as its costs and expenses. Taken together, the company's net income can be determined.

A company's ability to keep its doors open has a lot to do with how much money it is making. In order to **fund IT programs** and provide an IT team with the funding that they'll need in order to both start and complete projects, a company needs to have enough net income. IT managers who are able to determine the company's fiscal health using its income statement will be able to determine how best to guide their IT teams.

Chapter 8

IT Managers Need To Understand What A Cash Flow Statement Is

```
                            Aspring
        Cash flow statement for the year ended 31 December 20X9

                                              $           $
Cash flow from operating activities
  Profit before tax (21,000 - 17,000)       4,000
  Depreciation (10,000 - 8,000)             2,000
  Increase in inventories                  (3,500)
  Increase in receivables                  (5,000)
  Increase in payables                      1,000
Net cash outflow from operating activities            (1,500)

Cash flow from investing activities
  Payments to acquire non-current assets              (1,500)

Decrease in cash and cash equivalents                 (3,000)
Cash and cash equivalents at beginning of year         5,000

Cash and cash equivalents at end of year               2,000
```

Chapter 8: IT Managers Need To Understand What A Cash Flow Statement Is

In the world of high finance, there are three primary financial reports that your management will use to tell you how a firm is doing: income statement, balance statement, and the **cash flow statement**. An IT manager needs to be aware of what each of these reports contains and how to read them. The cash flow statement is one such report and, unfortunately, it's probably both the least used and least understood. Let's solve that problem right now...

What Is A Cash Flow Statement?

So before we dive in too deep, let's make sure that we all understand what we're talking about here. Just exactly what is a cash flow statement? The whole purpose behind a cash flow statement is to tell the reader why **the company's amount of cash changed**. How did the company get more cash and what happened to the cash that the company had?

A cash flow statement starts out by documenting how much cash the company had on hand at the start of the reporting period. Then, much like you probably do for your personal checking account, it goes through and documents how the company acquired and spent cash during the period. The final line in a cash flow statement is **how much cash the company had when the period came to a close**.

As an IT manager, your company's cash flow statement is important to you. The reason that you care is because when **you are preparing your budget for your IT dream team**, it could be quite helpful to take a look at the company's current cash flow projections. If the company is low on cash, then you'll want to limit the amount of funding that you request. However, if the company is swimming in cash, then you'll know that it's probably ok to ask for additional funding.

How Do You Read A Cash Flow Statement?

A cash flow statement has a lot to tell an IT manager. One of the most important things that you can determine by reading a cash flow statement is how successfully your company is able to turn accounts receivable (promises by customers to pay you) into cash. This is a critical piece of information to have because it will ultimately determine if your company is going to be able to **keep its doors open**.

There is **a simple equation** that you need to keep in mind when you are reading a cash flow statement:

Cash Flow from Profit + Other Sources of Cash – Uses of Cash = Change in Cash

An important point to realize is that the cash flow statement does not measure the same thing as the income statement. The key difference is that if there is **no cash transaction**, then it can't be reflected on the cash flow statement.

What Does All Of This Mean For You?

The cash flow statement is one of the **three primary financial statements** that are used to run a company. Because of its importance, IT managers need to make sure that they understand what a cash flow statement contains and how to read it.

A cash flow statement tells how much cash the company had on hand at the start of reporting period and how much it has on hand **at the end of the period**. The amount of cash that the company has at any point in time is of critical importance to an

IT manager because it will tell you if the company is going to be in a position to fund your requests for new projects, software, or hardware.

Reading a cash flow statement is not something that an IT manager is going to be sitting around doing every day. However, on a regular basis it is an activity that you should do – such as when your company issues its end of quarter or annual reports. Show some leadership and make sure that you understand how much money the company has on hand to fund projects and initiatives. This is the key to being able to explain to your team **just exactly what is going on** at your company.

Chapter 9

ROI: What It Is And Why IT Managers Need To Know How To Use It

Chapter 9: ROI: What It Is And Why IT Managers Need To Know How To Use It

In the world of IT we like to make up new acronyms all the time. Outsiders often don't fully understand what our acronyms stand for and so they feel like they don't know what's going on. Well guess what, other departments in your company can do the same thing and it will make you feel like **you don't know what's going on**. How about if we talk about ROI and what it really means…

What Is The Time Value Of Money?

Money is money, right? It comes as a bit of a surprise to many IT managers that **the value of money changes over time**. No, we're not talking about something complicated like inflation. Rather we're talking about one of the simplest concepts in finance that the rest of the company already knows.

It comes down to a very simple phrase that everyone already knows. "A dollar today is more valuable than a dollar tomorrow." What this means is that the longer that you have money in your hands, **the more valuable that money is** in comparison to money that someone has promised to give you at some point in time in the future.

In the world of business, the rest of the company likes to talk about what they can get money to do for them. In order to have conversations like this, they talk about what is called **the return on investment (ROI)** that they can get for the money that they have. A simple way to calculate ROI is to take a look at what you spent on something and then subtract that value from how much you ended up selling / making on the thing that you spent money on. The difference is often called the ROI.

How Do You Calculate A Return On Investment?

The problem with calculating ROI this way is that it's not really providing you with **a true estimate** of the return on your investment. The reason for this is because it fails to account for the timing of cash flows.

In order to calculate the true value of money by taking in the account of when you are getting that money, then you need to **provide some additional information**. You need to know 3 of the following four values in order to calculate the fourth value:

- **Present Value:** This is the value of the money that is being discussed today.

- **Future Value:** This is the value of the money that is being discussed at a specific point in time.

- **Periods:** This is the number of periods of time between now and when you want to measure the future value.

- **Rate:** This is the interest rate that you could get if you took the money today and put it in to an interest bearing savings account.

There are a number of different ways to **calculate this value**, the easiest way is to use a calculator, an Excel spreadsheet, or just use an online tool to calculate the value that you are looking for.

What Does All Of This Mean For You?

In order to be able to interact with other parts of the company, IT managers need to be able to **speak the same language that they do**. One important term that is used a great deal is Return On Investment (ROI).

Money has a different value depending on when you can get your hands on it. Money that you can get today is **more valuable** than money that you can get tomorrow. In order to be able to determine the value of money at any given point in time, you need to know how to calculate ROI. The correct calculation of an ROI requires that you know the present and future value of the money, the number of periods involved and the interest rate.

The company that you work for is always trying to get the most for its money. Because of that, it has **developed a vocabulary** around how it wants to talk about money.

As an IT manager, because you are part of the company, you need to **learn how to use the language** that the company uses to talk about the money that your IT team needs in order to do its work. This will include having a good understanding of what return on investment means and how to calculate it.

Most IT professionals don't know that much about the time value of money. Take the time to learn how to determine the true value of money at any point in time and **your value to the company will increase dramatically!**

Chapter 10

What Is Net Present Value And Why IT Managers Should Care About It?

DOW JONES INDUSTRIAL AVERAGE INDEX - Add to Portfolio - Discuss DJI

10,609.66
-449.36 (-4.06%)
Sep 17 - Close

Open: 11.056.58	Mkt Cap: -	P/E: -	Dividend: -
High: 11.057.31	52Wk High: 14.279.96	F P/E: -	Yield: -
Low: 10.595.90	52Wk Low: 10.595.90	Beta: -	Shares: -
Vol: 460.78M	Avg Vol: 205.20M	EPS: -	Inst. Own: -

Chapter 10: What Is Net Present Value And Why Should IT Managers Care About It?

The good news is that IT managers are often able to quickly wrap their heads around the concept that a dollar (or a euro, or a rand, or a…) in an IT budget that they are given today is more valuable than a dollar that they are given tomorrow. However, things get a bit more trickery when we try to determine **the net present value** of money that we might get tomorrow…

What Is Net Present Value?

So you may have heard **the term "NPV"** before, but just exactly what is it? The leadership of your company probably uses this term quite frequently, so you need to know all about it. In this case, perhaps an example would help you to understand it. Let's say that I come up to you and tell you that I'm going to give you US$1,000,000 five years from now. Hopefully, you'd be thrilled to hear that.

However, after a while you might start to think to yourself – hey, I really **don't want to wait 5 years** to get my hands on that money. I'd like to have it right now. Assuming that I was agreeable to giving you the money, I would not be willing to give you the full $1,000,000 – after all, that's how much I said that I'd give to you in 5 years, not today. In fact, I might not even have the $1,000,000 to give it to you today.

So **how much would I be willing to give to you?** Well, there are a lot of very good Net Present Value calculators on the Internet and they are easy to find. Assuming that you found one and that you also did some research and discovered that if you put money in the bank today and let it sit there, it would grow by 10% every year, then what you'd discover is that I should be willing to give you $620,000 today. The NPV calculations show that $620,000 over 5 years at a 10% interest rate will give you $1,000,000 in 5 years.

In a nutshell, that's what NPV is. It's simply **the present value** of a future sum. What you do to calculate the present value of a future payment is to discount the future payment at some annual compound interest rate.

How Can IT Managers Use Net Present Value?

So knowing what NPV is can be a powerful tool for any IT manager. However, the next question is **why do I need to know about this?** Ultimately what all of this comes down to is that NPV is a decision making tool that you can use when you are trying to make decisions about what your IT dream team should be working on.

One note, we refer to it as **"net present value"** (and not "present value") because when we are using it, after we calculate the present value we'll go ahead and subtract off any initial investment costs.

The question that you'll want to be asking yourself when you are using NPV is if the initial investment that you'd have to make in an IT project would be worth **the future benefit** that the project will deliver.

Using the numbers that we calculated above, if the initial startup costs for an IT project were $650,000 and the project would result in savings to the company of $1,000,000 in 5 years, then the answer would be no – the investment in doing the project **would not be worth it**.

What Does All Of This Mean For You?

Net Present Value (or NPV) is **a financial tool** that IT managers can use during budgeting and project planning processes to help with their discussions with company management. NPV tells an IT manager what the current value of money that they'll receive in the future is.

The value of knowing this amount is that it can help in **the decision making process**. When planning an IT project, the use of NPV can help an IT manager make the decision as to if spending IT budget dollars on this project is the best use of limited IT funds.

NPV is a simple financial concept that the rest of the company uses every day. IT managers need to understand what NPV is and how to use it in order to be able to successfully communicate **their funding needs** and plans with the rest of the company.

Chapter 11

Internal Rate Of Return (IRR): Why IT Managers Should Know How To Use It

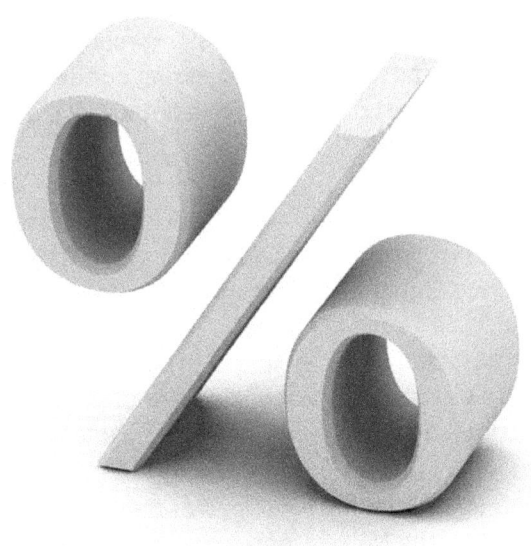

Chapter 11: Internal Rate Of Return (IRR): Why IT Managers Should Know How To Use It

As an IT manager you will eventually be responsible for convincing your company to fund an IT project that your IT dream team wants to work on. Sure, from a technology point-of-view this may be a necessary project to do; however, the leadership in your company who control the funding **probably don't really care about that** – they want to know how much money the company is going to make if you do this project.

What Is The Internal Rate Of Return (IRR)?

The question that the rest of the company is going to be asking you about the IT project that you are requesting funding for will be **"...is this the best thing for us to be spending our limited funds on?"** It's a good question and you had better have a good answer for it.

It turns out that there is a standard way of talking about the value of a project. The Internal Rate Of Return (IRR) is **a time-value tool** that allows IT managers to make a decision as to if a proposed IT project is a good idea or not. If you are faced with having to choose between multiple possible IT projects, then IRR can help you to pick the one that will deliver the best benefits for the company.

In formal business-speak, the IRR is defined as being **the discount rate** at which the Net Present Value (NPV) of an investment equals zero. This is just a fancy way of answering the question "How much money will this project generate for the company over time?"

Yes, you could calculate this by hand, but it would take quite some time. Instead, this is the type of calculation that you need to do using either a fancy calculator or, even better, a spreadsheet. The % that you'll get is the return on **every dollar that the company chooses to invest into the project**.

What Is The Hurdle Rate?

Making a positive return on every dollar that it invests into your IT project sounds wonderful for the company, doesn't it? However, that's not going to be enough to get your project funded. For you see, the company has a lot of other things that it can do with its money and they too will generate a return on every dollar that they invest in it. **Where should they spend their money?**

It turns out that there is a simple way to determine if the IRR value associated with your project is good enough to cause it to be funded. Every company has a value that they called **the hurdle rate**. This is a percentage that is the minimum rate of return that all investments that the company makes must achieve.

The thinking behind this is pretty simple. In the worst case, the company could take all of its investment money and stick it in a bank savings account. If they did this, then they would be guaranteed to earn a certain amount of money at the end of a period of time. You want them to invest in your project. That means that you've got to be able to show that your project is going to be able to generate enough money to cover what the company would earn if they just put their money in the bank **along with extra money to compensate the company for the risk that they'll be taking by investing in your risky project.**

What Does All Of This Mean For You?

Nobody ever said that being an IT manager was going to be an easy job! You are going to be called on to **present IT projects for funding approval** to your company's management. When you do this, you need to be ready to talk about the project using the terms that the rest of the company uses.

Internal Rate Of Return (IRR) is one such term. The IRR is a percentage value that tells the rest of the company how much money an investment in your project would generate. Knowing this value, decisions can be made between **multiple different ways** to spend the company's money.

Even if you don't anticipate that you'll be asked to provide an IRR during a request for project funding, **it might still be a good idea to** calculate **it**. During heated funding discussions, it's always a good idea to have standardized values available to add credibility to your request during the discussion. Good luck!

Chapter 12

---

3 Financial Terms That IT Managers Need To Know

Chapter 12: 3 Financial Terms That IT Managers Need To Know

What makes an IT manager successful? In a word it's communication. The IT managers who are able to successfully reach out and talk with the rest of the business using terms that they use every day are the ones who will be able to **get more things done with their IT dream team and get them done quicker**. In order for you to be considered to be a successful IT manager, you are going to have to boost your vocabulary by learning and understanding what the following three financial terms mean.

Fixed Costs

Your company makes something. It can be a real physical product – something that you can touch and feel. Or perhaps it is a service. No matter, in creating the "thing" that your company sells, there are all sorts of costs associated with making each unit of it. One such type of cost is called the **"fixed costs"**.

These are the types of costs that are going to **stay pretty much the same** no matter how many units of your company's product get manufactured. These costs can include such things as rent or lease payments, insurance, and salaries. As an example: the amount of rent that the company has to pay will remain the same no matter if the company makes one unit or 100,000 units.

Variable Costs

Variable costs are where things start to get interesting. IT managers will often hear their leadership talking about company plans that are designed to find ways to **manage or reduce variable costs** throughout the company.

Variable costs are the costs that **will change based on the number of units that the company decides to produce and sell**. Good examples of variable costs can include labor costs, raw material costs, and the cost of utilities. It all comes down to one simple fact: the more units that the company makes, the more of these items it will consume.

Contribution Margin

All of those costs have to be paid for somehow. Ultimately it comes down to creating products and selling those products in order to make enough money for the company to pay off its fixed and variable costs.

The contribution margin tells the company **how much of its fixed costs** are going to be paid off by selling each unit. Here's how contribution margin is defined:

net unit revenue – variable costs per unit

What All Of This Means For You

In the world of IT in which we all live in, it can be very easy to slide into just having discussions with our fellow IT workers using the IT vocabulary that seems to be almost second-nature to us. We need to take the time and the effort to **learn how best to communicate with the rest of the company** using the terms that they use every day.

A great place to start leaning what terms to use is to **master the use of fixed costs, variable costs, and contribution margin**. These three terms all relate to the costs that the company faces when it creates each individual unit of product that it hopes to sell. When the company has to make decisions about what it wants to do next, these are the terms that it uses to consider its options.

As an IT manager, if you both know what these terms mean and if you are comfortable using them, then you'll be ready to participate in **the company's important management planning discussions**. You have a lot of IT knowledge that the company needs, make sure that you also have the vocabulary so that you can share what you know with the rest of the company...!

It's from the forge of failure that the steel of success is formed.

Hard Work Does Not Guarantee Success, But Success Does Not Happen Without Hard Work.

- Dr. Jim Anderson

Create IT Departments That Are Productive And A Valuable Asset To The Rest Of The Company !

Dr. Jim Anderson is available to provide training and coaching on the topics that are the most important to people who have to manage IT departments: how can I build a productive IT department (and keep it together) while at the same time providing the rest of the company with the IT services that they need?

Dr. Anderson believes that in order to both learn and remember what he says, speakers need to laugh. Each one of his speeches is full of fun and humor so that what he says "sticks" with everyone.

Dr. Anderson's CIO SkillsTraining Includes:

1. How to identify and attract the right type of IT workers to your IT department.
2. How to build relationships with the company's senior management in order to get the support that you need?
3. How to stay on top of changing technology and security issues so that you never get surprised?

Dr. Jim Anderson works with over 100 customers per year. To invite Dr. Anderson to work with you, contact him at:

Phone: 813-418-6970 or
Email: jim@BlueElephantConsulting.com

Blue
Elephant
Consulting
Speaking Negotiating Managing Marketing

10

Photo Credits:

Cover - By: GotCredit
https://www.flickr.com/photos/jakerust/

Chapter 1 - By: 401(K) 2012
https://www.flickr.com/photos/68751915@N05/

Chapter 2 – By: 401(K) 2012
https://www.flickr.com/photos/68751915@N05/

Chapter 3 – By: Philippe Put
https://www.flickr.com/photos/34547181@N00/

Chapter 4 – By: The JR James Archive
https://www.flickr.com/photos/jrjamesarchive/

Chapter 5 – By: Blatant World
https://www.flickr.com/photos/blatantworld/

Chapter 6 – By: Brightworks
https://www.flickr.com/photos/sfbrightworks/

Chapter 7 – By: Trianons Oficial
https://www.flickr.com/photos/trianons/

Chapter 8 – By: online free accounting
https://www.flickr.com/photos/50637698@N08/

Chapter 9 – By: Wall Street Investing Group
https://www.flickr.com/photos/wallstreetinvestinggroup/

Chapter 10 – By: YoTuT
https://www.flickr.com/photos/yotut/

Chapter 11 – By: allthingsqb.com
http://allthingsqb.com

Chapter 12 – By: 401(K) 2012
https://www.flickr.com/photos/68751915@N05/

Other Books By The Author

Product Management

- Product Management Secrets: Techniques For Product Managers To Boost Product Sales And Increase Customer Satisfaction

- Product Development Lessons For Product Managers: How Product Managers Can Create Successful Products

- Customer Lessons For Product Managers: Techniques For Product Managers To Better Understand What Their Customers Really Want

- Product Failure Lessons For Product Managers: Examples Of Products That Have Failed For Product Managers To Learn From

- Communication Skills For Product Managers: The Communication Skills That Product Managers Need To Know How To Use In Order To Have A Successful Product

- How To Have A Successful Product Manager Career: The Things That You Need To Be Doing TODAY In Order To Have A Successful Product Manager Career

- Product Manager Product Success: How to keep your product on track and make it become a success

Public Speaking

- Secrets To Organizing A Speech For Maximum Impact: How to put together a speech that will capture and hold your audience's attention

- How To Become A Better Speaker By Changing How You Speak: Change techniques that will transform a speech into a memorable event

- How To Give A Great Presentation: Presentation techniques that will transform a speech into a memorable event

- How To Rehearse In Order To Give The Perfect Speech: How to effectively rehearse your next speech to that your message be remembered forever!

- Secrets To Creating The Perfect Speech: How to create a speech that will make your message be remembered forever!

- Secrets To Organizing The Perfect Speech: How to organize the best speech of your life!

- Secrets To Planning The Perfect Speech: How to plan to give the best speech of your life

- How To Show What You Mean During A Presentation: How to use visual techniques to transform a speech into a memorable event

CIO Skills

- What CIOs Need To Know About Working With Partners: Techniques For CIOs To Use In Order To Be Able To Successfully Work With Partners

- Critical CIO Management Skills: Decision Making Skills That Every CIO Needs To Have In Order To Be Able To Make The Right Choices

- How CIOs Can Make Innovation Happen: Tips And Techniques For CIOs To Use In Order To Make Innovation Happen In Their IT Department

- CIO Communication Skills Secrets: Tips And Techniques For CIOs To Use In Order To Become Better Communicators

- Managing Your CIO Career: Steps That CIOs Have To Take In Order To Have A Long And Successful Career

- CIO Business Skills: How CIOs can work effectively with the rest of the company!

IT Manager Skills

- Growing Your CIO Career: How CIOs Can Work With The Entire Company In Order To Be Successful

- How IT Managers Can Make Innovation Happen: Tips And Techniques For IT Managers To Use In Order To Make Innovation Happen In Their Teams

- Staffing Skills IT Managers Must Have: Tips And Techniques That IT Managers Can Use In Order To Correctly Staff Their Teams

- Secrets Of Effective Leadership For IT Managers: Tips And Techniques That IT Managers Can Use In Order To Develop Leadership Skills

- IT Manager Career Secrets: Tips And Techniques That IT Managers Can Use In Order To Have A Successful Career

- IT Manager Budgeting Skills: How IT Managers Can Request, Manage, Use, And Track Their Funding

Negotiating

- Learn How To Signal In Your Next Negotiation: How To Develop The Skill Of Effective Signaling In A Negotiation In Order To Get The Best Possible Outcome

- Learn The Skill Of Exploring In A Negotiation: How To Develop The Skill Of Exploring What Is Possible In A Negotiation In Order To Reach The Best Possible Deal

- Learn How To Argue In Your Next Negotiation: How To Develop The Skill Of Effective Arguing In A Negotiation In Order To Get The Best Possible Outcome

- How To Open Your Next Negotiation: How To Start A Negotiation In Order To Get The Best Possible Outcome

- Preparing For Your Next Negotiation: What You Need To Do BEFORE A Negotiation Starts In Order To Get The Best Possible Deal

- Learn How To Package Trades In Your Next Negotiation

Miscellaneous

- The Internet-Enabled Successful School District Superintendent: How To Use The Internet To Boost Parental Involvement In Your Schools

- Power Distribution Unit (PDU) Secrets: What Everyone Who Works In A Data Center Needs To Know!

- Making The Jump: How To Land Your Dream Job When You Get Out Of College!

- How To Use The Internet To Create Successful Students And Involved Parents

"What IT Managers Need To Know In Order To Understand How Their Company Uses Money"

This book has been written with one goal in mind – to show you how an IT manager can successfully manage their budget. It's not easy being an IT manager so we're going to show you what you need to be doing in order to request, manage, use and track your budget successfully!

Let's Make Your IT budget A Success!

<u>**What You'll Find Inside:**</u>

- **WHY IT MANAGERS NEED TO CARE ABOUT FINANCIAL STATEMENTS**

- **AN IT MANAGER'S NEW BEST FRIEND: THE COMPANY BALANCE SHEET**

- **ROI: WHAT IT IS AND WHY IT MANAGERS NEED TO KNOW HOW TO USE IT**

- **3 FINANCIAL TERMS THAT IT MANAGERS NEED TO KNOW**

Dr. Jim Anderson brings his 25 years of real-world experience to this book. He's been an IT manager at some of the world's largest firms. He's going to show you what you need to do (and not do!) in order to successfully manage your IT budget!

www.ingramcontent.com/pod-product-compliance
Lightning Source LLC
Chambersburg PA
CBHW070935180526
45168CB00003B/1081